# My Notes

# My Notes

# My Notes

# My Notes

# My Notes

# My Notes

# My Notes

# My Notes

# My Notes

# My Notes

# My Notes

# My Notes

## My Notes

## My Notes

# My Notes

# My Notes

# My Notes

## My Notes

# My Notes

# My Notes

# My Notes

# My Notes

# My Notes

# My Notes

# My Notes

# My Notes

# My Notes

# My Notes

# My Notes

# My Notes

# My Notes

# My Notes

# My Notes

# My Notes

# My Notes

# My Notes

# My Notes

# My Notes

# My Notes

# My Notes

# My Notes

# My Notes

# My Notes

# My Notes

# My Notes

# My Notes

# My Notes

# My Notes

# My Notes

# My Notes

# My Notes

# My Notes

# My Notes

# My Notes

# My Notes

# My Notes

# My Notes

# My Notes

# My Notes

## My Notes

# My Notes

# My Notes

# My Notes

# My Notes

# My Notes

# My Notes

# My Notes

# My Notes

# My Notes

# My Notes

# My Notes

# My Notes

# My Notes

# My Notes

# My Notes

# My Notes

# My Notes

# My Notes

# My Notes

## My Notes

# My Notes

# My Notes

# My Notes

# My Notes

# My Notes

# My Notes

# My Notes

# My Notes

# My Notes

## My Notes

# My Notes

# My Notes

# My Notes

# My Notes

# My Notes

# My Notes

# My Notes

# My Notes

# My Notes

# My Notes

# My Notes

# My Notes

## My Notes

# My Notes

# My Notes

# My Notes

# My Notes

# My Notes

# My Notes

# My Notes

# My Notes

# My Notes

# My Notes

# My Notes

# My Notes

# My Notes

# My Notes

# My Notes

# My Notes

# My Notes

www.ingramcontent.com/pod-product-compliance
Lightning Source LLC
LaVergne TN
LVHW012118070526
838202LV00056B/5776